Good News for Immediate Release

The Silver Lining of the 45th President
(Everyone has one and that is
good but what else is behind it?)

This book is non-fiction

This is not only a Christian affair,
it is a humanitarian affair!

This is the time that the greatest destruction of our land and our principles for which we stand has ever been put to the test of trying to create the destruction of America. If we don't do something about it we can't blame anyone but ourselves. I do need to say more about how the so call earthly commander and chief of the USA is doing.

About the author
It is real

This may be one of the books I authored that may seem like it has madness and a little craziness in it but by the time you get to the end it will all make sense.

Dedicated to the American Public

Copyright 2018

1

I don't know if it is a sad thing or glad thing for people to know that I fought with demons of my own as I wrote my way out of darkness also. I am someone who is still a work in progress but I have come a long way and you can go a long way also.

To relate to everyone who joins in on the peaceful revelation, you are the phenomenons of the world to identify with what we can do as one in the holy assembly of Christ Jesus.

Therapy

This country hasn't had any real great news in a while, until now. Here is our big chance to make things better. They talk about all of the garbage that is going on but when is the last time you heard any real news that may have come straight from the Lord himself? It has landed on the planet and mankind is supposed to take heed to it. I think it is time we receive the message from the Lord and his instructions of how to improve and change before we are more so falling into a devastating state of existence.

To the public at large: this is a PSA to inform you that there is an inoculation available to anyone who has been bitten by the trumpitis bug. Now they are able to get a trumpectomy.

This is a consideration that the Holy Spirit has brought forward in order for anyone to be freed from the attraction and the magnetism that towerists have that draws people to them in a way that gives them an advantage over their conscious way of thinking and basically has a power and control over their balance of reality. We are offering this information so that someone can get free from this attraction which happens to be President Trump.

I personally have no problem with anyone who wants to vote for Mr. Trump because that is their preference and their right.

I have been given the job to assure that no one has been taken advantage of or no one has the perception that does not really exist of a certain person. Additionally, to assure that no one has to regret that they made a mistake by voting for someone who they thought was someone else and they weren't. This is done by way of a free gift from the Holy Spirit to make sure that we can have a fair and impartial election because, at present, it may not be that way. We want justice to prevail as a citizen of the body of Christ and a citizen of the American public and the United States.

This can be called spiritual help

The thing about this inoculation or vaccination is it is painless, odorless and harmless. It only enhances the sensibilities of developing the awareness of the positive energy that they have within that can also become lost or misguided or even mistreated and this is a fact of life. What this inoculation does is free someone from a bondage of being under those types of negative influences so they can outgrow the presence of anything that can influence them in the wrong way.

3

This is only a personal opinion. I feel that we as a member of the body of Christ and a nation of people need to understand how to be more open-minded and liberal in our judgment on who we choose to help run our society, either up the ladder toward successful opportunities whether they are Democrat or Republican or any other party.

We have to choose the best person for the job not just a title or label or someone who is of another dimension who has the razzmatazz and makes you feel so much jazz about them that you get behind them and try to be a part of their yocky-dock, witchcraft or voodooism because they have some kind of enchanting spell.

If we can captivate a new level of spiritual peace that we can share, it is our duty to share and that is one of the latest writings I have done for all who may be dissatisfied with the newly elected president and his administration. I am the author of other books that numbers many.

The latest may be one of the greatest ways to help all people get through the next few years and make the kind of gain in the lives of people that money can't buy.

It is filled with a wealth of wisdom that was inspired by the Holy Spirit to be written and presented to show a new way to utilize the power of love. Let everyone know how much better it makes you feel. We can help the state of our country's development within the will of the Lord because it doesn't have to be a kind of drought over the next few years when things can still be fruitful within our nation.

Anything that can draw people closer to the Lord should be embellished as priceless!

We are hoping that the leaders of the congregations help to promote one or more of these books. We are asking in the name of the Lord. It will help us continue the work we are doing and we can keep releasing the other books that are being publishing.

Your help is needed to stop the country from shortchanging itself from the blessings it has to come! The top and bottom of this is the Lord has blessed America now it is time for America to bless the Lord, and the house of God's people need to be first to do this.

The time has come to put a stop to one of Satan's strongholds that he has on mankind. It is a place of a kind of unawareness that takes and captures them. It is the unfamiliar state of towerism. It is a blinding force that needs to be reckoned with on a Godly level.

A Way is in the Books

This is a renewal plan for people, the country and the world showing that the Lord still forgives us so we can make things better.

When all is read and done

Your faith will cleanse you so you can enter a new atmosphere within to be able to walk in righteousness in the spiritual wisdom of the Lord.

This new book helps to redefine, re-correlate and recalculate the American spirit. It helps show new ways to add light to what may be a pathway that holds a kind of darkness that is misplaced that needs to be seen before people walk onto it, whether it is a day from now or years from now or how it came about.

One of our number one goals is to get to as many people as we can that have towerism and get them to get a towerectomy if they are stuck like the 45th president. This sickness that is of a spiritual origin can be cured. It will make the world a better place. It will stop lots of mankind's destruction. Keeping in mind one thing, people need to change the fact of giving up their free will for the Lord's will in their life.

The fact of the matter is when people got stopped from building the Tower of Babel, they got mad and sad. The DNA of this spiritual problem went forth to curse mankind and it has disappeared to the naked eye but not to the spirit that exists in mankind and has done more damage than it should have done. Now the Lord says stop it. It's to be know as towerism and our 45th president has it.

One of the biggest benefits of understanding this is we have learned it can bless mankind. Also, it is people approved and is a kind of illness that the prescription does not have to be FDA approved because it is already approved by the Lord.

At the time of this writing, Les Moonves was the latest titan towerist to fall; thank God. This is ungodly power being used for abuse.

The dieconomie book The lady police who shot the man in his house is the latest public person to get caught up in Satan's dieconomie. Can this be another level of towerism? It kills and destroys.

This is the biggies

What was the biggest thing no. 45 did? It was to expose his kind of towerism in the political and private arenas, no question about.

People please try to understand this is not capitalism but towerism: two different kinds of people.

It is time for the power that was taken from those who seemed powerless to be restored.

The development of the therapy that is in the books give a cure to a lot of people superstitious hoodoo and voodoo within people that think exist that leads to people to void-noid numb-dumb sin-drome.

Let the people know that the #metoo movement has not died out and the fact that so many outdated politicians are staying in the way and some are even womanizers that are remaining in office, political and others. This must stop today to ignore the people who are doing wrong thins and somewhat getting away with it. That is why this is the #usedtoo movement.

Now that we understand the principles and the concepts how do we votes and make them think or believe it is their own idea or just believe in what is right by using the make people greater than they are now moving by or with giving them spiritual grit that may not have to learn about the skills that creates a whole host of pattern to grow from.

We are talking about no. 45

Let them know if it wasn't for other reasons and the Russians he wouldn't be in office along with the fact that there needs to be a stop put to all the controversies in the government because it is a blinding force that creates a dark side to the presence of America. That has been a problem all along but it is time it came to a head as it has but it needs to stop. We don't need the unknown presence of any kind of darkness looming over the country and if you don't feel it, it is because you don't have enough of the spirituality that gives a way out to people.

Now this alert is out and the main reason is we have a kind of bully in the White House also and this could be good in ways but not so good in others. The fact that this country had to become a bullet bully shows us that we got to know when to hold them and know when to fold them like a game of chance we don't need to take a chance with keeping the trump card any longer. His hand needs to be folded and put out of the White House, table closed because no one needs the art of the deal any longer, thanks to the majesty of the will of the Lord being presented.

If someone learns to do this beforehand then it wouldn't happen as often. It is also the way to help stop childhood bullying to forgive in a divine order of love that helps to stop Satan's dieconomie. If Cain forgave either way he wouldn't have killed Abel. The fruit of the tree would become null and void. Forgive one's self for thinking wrong to stop the seed and action.

At BTHPM, we have completely unlocked a part of the reason that causes death to help stop the killing.

Why is this so hard to do? For some, it is because they need to understand the darkness. This will make it not so simple but simple at the same time. That gives them a way out of the darkness of a maze at the time that is needed every time it is needed to be known.

We can acknowledge the people who voted for Trump and then let them know what is going on. You can't change their vote but you can help them make up their mind to not do it again.

There is a fact that towerists are and have been a big part of this country starting as slave owners and then they put their less fortunate or uneducated people on a slave wage level and then on a lie to blind them level to take their vote so they still can steal and rob them blind as their own wealth grew.

One way out

The old way of action is on a level of how the West was won and anyone can be a bullet bully in life with a gun and that is the Tommy gun way of thinking on the gangster way of negativity. That can change.

It is now so old and outdated only a fool lives by it's principles. So get out of a state of mind that reflects bad history and news and if you want to live learn to kill someone with love even if it calls for you to leave them at the altar.

Does this have something to do with existentialism or is it the opposite of an existentialist that we are known as?

To get down to the bottom of what is going on in America, there has not been a president like Trump in the White House who has caused as many political wars since forever and that is one of the most dangerous things for the USA. It causes us to have divided ways and this is an unhealthy state of life.

If you don't know it if you take any nation that is going through some kind of hell, it starts off with the government and it falls onto the people. It is a fact now how to avoid or change it. It has been written in _The Book of No Lies_ can help stop the dictators and tyrants who are also towerists.

There is some work cut out for us. In many ways in this book I have written the plan that the spirit of the Lord in me has given the answers to make the things in life that we are facing better. This will keep mankind in a bounty of love so all can know the loveoutame angels that are in us all.

If I can go this far with a some what 4th grade formal education from mankind and the rest of what I learned was by experience also in the theology school I was taken into at no charge by Pastor Ribbins, a great man of God. I love because he and others wanted me there even if I couldn't pay for it. This is why I feel so good about trying to give back when I can.

To help people who may be going through GPTSD, the book *Calm During the Storm* can also help. It was written to help create revelation because when some people get trapped in the wilderness they go a little buck wild and are off balance to help not get that way and most of all teach them to stop liking raise hell. That is one of the reason why this was written.

This may not be as much pain as some may think to gain the self-worth back you may have lost by us not using our vote the right way.

We will also be able to escape the spiritual warfare that is caused by the separation of people that is a problem the government may be caused also. It is an outdated system. Does a lot of this come about because of political wars? I think so that is why when we help ourselves we help them.

To all: how can this process go viral to help as many people as needed. It is for the more fortunate people to put the word out to know even more, check the book because the more you know the less the storm shows up along with the GPTSD that we can help end with another book, _Ending Political Wars_. It is available to help and add to God's therapy.

Congratulations to all who voted for
the 45th president of the USA

This is a kind of congratulation manual to all who voted for the 45th president, but If you plan to do it again.

The books that are referred to in this manual are available for purchase online at Createspace store (paperback) or Amazon.com (eBook):

M N

If no. 45 gets in again it will be harder to come back because it may be a setback of up to 40 years.

If we don't get our house in order we might as well stop trying to tell others how to get theirs right because no one will pay us any attention.

The world is starting to not respect America

Moses was a great man of God who led the people out of Egypt but they wandered in the wilderness for 40 years. Think of what no. 45 will do if we let him lead us any longer. God only knows how many may miss the right eternity because of this kind of mess.

It is time to bypass this kind of highway to a make believe kind of heaven on earth that no. 45 portrays.

In Jesus' name I pray you see the picture that does need to be completed with your help because together we stand and divided we fall can you take this to heart. It will tell you the truth.

Some of The mottoes of BTHPM

Don't let your vote get hung up on a tree in the place of us because it is almost the same as it being a person because it hangs the future in limbo of the youth and people of America.

Is defeating the people by not having them come out to vote like a new kind of way to keep people in charge or worse a bondage of man-made proportions that limited the way we can live?

The wisdom of it all we can now consider this series of books God's prevention of therapy to stop and or head off the re-defended deliverance from man-made disasters that helps to give relief for nations of people with the Government Post Traumatic Stress Depression/Disorder (GTPSD) order that causes rioting and makes people of other countries sometimes go to war with other people as it has done in the land which we live in. This may have all came about because of the wrong laws put in place that made a man made disaster.

It is time to stop then renew your vows with the Lord as the watchmen and women of the people at home and the world to get a new process of living and using the heart to think more and not the mind.

Bad news that can change

The government PTSD is causing people stress, anxiety, depression, hopelessness and the stress of the nations full of the destitute, lost and service men and women's families. It has been doing this but the other part of it is people who have been rioting and fighting that breaks out at rallies and protest gatherings.

Does this increase crime? What do you think?

This is some of the things people have witnessed. The unseen things are the abuse that happens at homes and maybe some of the suicide and crime. It is a crisis in America the facts stands for it all. That is why this Christ-like message has shown up to take down the ungodliness.

If the government had a better plan to show love the less harm it can do to the country that looks up to it. Now how many servants of the government are crooks in disguise.

This writing is a part of one or more of the books I have authored to help bring understanding that helps with the new news in this book.

There are so many ways to try to explain the synopsis for this new book. I hope you can connect with this; it may be somewhat lengthy; I thank you for your time.

Some information came out of books I authored

Before the RNC/DNC book was completed there was a plan put together to help the elected officials in Washington DC to get a grip on what was and is going on in the different levels of DC and throughout the whole political arena in the USA.

I still haven't released it but it will be presented to them once I get to a comfortable state of reflecting on what we at BTHPM are informing the people in America about that will help to improve the nation's well being and help stop the separation on all levels.

Introduction to the DNC/RNC

The books are a presentation of information that presents a foresight that is a gift to mankind by way of the Holy Spirit that has been tested by human hands and written by the hand that was given the blueprint to help create peace at the upcoming presidential election on both the Democratic and Republican parties in order to have as good or better outcome as was with the people and police because of the love that shines through that gave everyone a presence of stability and civility. It will be done using the same messages to help manage the presence of non-violence.

This prescription gives a nation time to get its vaccination so the ungodly unruliness can't become a part of the movement to keep the well being of all people first.

The greatest part about all of this is it becomes something like a play that is unfolding in front of the rest of the world and we can be on our best behavior now that rehearsal has given us a passing grade to give more incentive. On top of that the three rulers that make up your home run has been presented in a phase of work that took over forty years to bring forth one incident one day at a time when it is most needed, thanks to the Lord. That includes the things that amount to the loveoutame process.

Now is not the time to have reservations or fear that causes disruption in our lives as Americans we can still be known as the leader of the free world. If you are not on board then leave the country and let us get back on track in order that it may one day help you also wherever you go.

The fact still remains that there hasn't been a complete program put in place for so many communities in the USA. They still have not figured out how to address the problems of people who need to stop the development of a resurgence in themselves in order to be able to accept the change or be a part of the change. Instead, they want to be a part of destructive factors of the change to stop.

So many young people will continue the negative process of wanting to tear down, destroy, rob, kill, use drugs and not have the right goals set in place to also be made equipped to accept the new challenges because they have been put into a state of negativity and have developed traits which need to be redeveloped and new positive traits need to be infused within them.

Today if this new projects get to the forefront it is a way to start and kick off a way to help the inner city start up. We need to see if the people in the country and Washington are already committed.

Next could the unknown GPTSD cause people to contract towerism? Could the people who work there also got infested by it? Is this a sickness of a new kind that help to make some of the people ill? Does a part of the public at large get affected? Is this a part of people's unknown problems?

Does this mess up the silver lining in people,
more so youth?

Does this cripple us from seeing the high definition in what is supposed to be a leader? Many people get disgruntled over how they feel. But can we just look at other countries and get a hint? We do not want to end up like them even if we do not do anything about it and can it have a more devastating affect. When it comes to America there are many who are able to be saved by the Lord. So if you do not get behind get behind this for this reason alone: The Lord will be more pleased with you more for it, check mate!

The bottom line is how much of the government's PTSD from their process of dysfunction does it cause others to have this illness that needs to be corrected? Whatever the numbers are we need to work on them and correct them so we do not lose a generation. I think this was also a problem for past generations that we may have lost because we did not have a correct sense of social and economic development that checks on it because we were blind to Satan sitting up in a high place as a towerist in government.

Not good but true

The country was built off of people who were bullet bullies the culture of America was the same but life was made from people that the Lord made from his love. Love power can stop the presence of anyone being a bullet bully in life, no matter who they are.

I may have insight about some things but not all things. That is why I write on some of the things to give balance to what I say as if there were an upset of the Donald getting in the White House again for four more years. Is it possible that the opposition gets upset and act a fool?

God forbid but whoever has the win we should be ready for one thing that is to not act a fool as a member of the USA along with the fact that if there is a chance that the ungodly ways of some don't find a way to hack into any part of our presence regardless to what level of democracy it is.

To add to the help

In preparation for the future I intend to check to see whether or not I will be able to release the books again and make them free to the public as eBooks as I did before. During the upcoming election in 2020 hopefully I will have the complete attention of the country by then so they will all be able to receive the information within the books.

What I have planned is to release the eBooks aging before the next RNC/DNC. I want to make sure that it is known throughout the nation. Hopefully this will be done at the right time that will be determined soon before it is needed. This will help decrease the amount of violence in America to help the country become alert so good things can come our way!

This one of the Lord's super duper way to help us

Putting together the right systematic plan to not take the wind out of the sails of the president because he may trying to find the good in him self and it would not be hard to do if the Lord requires us help to because if he wants us to stay under this kind of bondage because of our disobedience as American people, we will. I think we need to become more thankful and do this in truth.

What is the deal with the attraction to no. 45? Lots of people want to know how they can basically become wheelers or dealers. This may be one of Satan's tools that he uses against people to keep them in towers. Some do the destruction they do in ways that may not be seen at first. We have to turn this kind of polarity around where they do not want to (but need to) go because it is not healthy for them. It puts people under a kind of spell that is somewhat related to a gloomy zombie state of not thinking clearly, because of a selfish inner atmosphere not meaning to offend anyone by saying this but I have been there from following a towerist and almost lost my life because of it. Some feel if they follow people they may be like them. That is the reason it is said to be careful what you may wish for.

When you take a good look

We do not have to try to make ourselves a legend in our own minds if we know the Lord is.

The less attractive it becomes it is the deception of a reality it places upon people, the less people will want to be a part of it. Because of this we can help give them a trumpectomy to free them and it do just that.

Let's see Mr. Trump for who he really is: a man with a sometimes foolish tweeting plan who is trying to ignore mankind for his own general purposes and reality not forgetting how he loves to make the rich richer and the poor poorer. The book _Fixing What is Broken in America by Stopping Towerism_ can explain more about this so we are not on the front line by ourselves and this help knowing we are not alone.

This projects helps them with being on the inside as a towerist looking on the outside as a people. What they do when they look in the mirror gives them a reflection of themselves and what they could become. Who wants to be like that who has any common sense and spiritual virtue in this reality and spiritual skills ability? No one except someone who is foolish and ignorant to what God has for them in the end because what they gain now doesn't mean anything because when they leave here it won't do them any good.

These are the principles that must be relayed to them to help free them from bondage. More so now to forever stop the process as all need to stop becoming a towerist and not trap.

The greatest thing that can be done during the course of this process is we can help free them from wanting to create violence and teach them a new kind of propaganda that he is not about which is peace and not the violence that he has declared and he wants to share because of his confusion and his reality.

The man is trapped like a dirty bird that sits in a cage in a tower who can't get enough feed. All he wants to do is crap down on people. That is how lots of them are when the truth is told. They can fake the funk but their reality is of a selfish greed and wanting to succeed so badly that it makes no difference how others feel.

The truth about someone who is almost 100% a towerist is they think other individuals are less than them so they move others out of the way and take things that they believe is their own (or they are entitled to). They forget about Godly morals and humanitarian values. That is why we can help take them down in a good way so they can stop making some others look like a clown. That is what they think of us as, court jesters or clowns. Look at the line that is now behind him and at one time was beside him who are falling. I am referring to no. 45.

It is time for them to recognize that they can't keep
thinking of us as peons or slaves of some kind
because we are the sons and daughters of the King.
We are not the peons that we may have allowed
ourselves in the position of by way of being lost in the
inner perspective of missing self-reliance and self-
worth that we may have needed to have.

The good news

The dawning of this new day is here and the freedom
that is getting ready to take place is an
unprecedented event that we must share in through
this foresight so we won't be behind looking like a
jackass.

A better day to come for some

Who do we share this with? everyone because it is
free to all in need and even after the election is over if
you think someone needs it give it to them and don't
ignore yourself if you are in need because lots of
people deny a problem with self all of the time.

Denying a bad future in our presence

What maybe the good side of not giving some of the
people four more years of this president no. 45 may
create a factor that leaves us with forty years to clean
up the massive mess made and left by one person
and a group of I can't say the word I have in mind that
has no resistance to let him do whatever he wanted to
do. So let's take a look forward and in the years to

come, would the country and the world be able to take this president that is a kind of tweety who loves Twitter? I say this because it is going to take that long to clear up the issues he has caused already, maybe it will be between four to eight years. This could be an estimated state of just my thinking.

The reason I say this is he may take up to 20 to 40 years on more of history and completely knocked it off its pedestal to the level of a 50-60% margin that is left. He also knocked anywhere from 20-30% of the country's level off personal balance in the development of history off of the pendulum that has to be restructured, redone and replaced that is here in the USA also across the world. It is like what you may stop that could have been done.

The equation that I am lost in may have needed a level of only shaking up the RNC/DNC to help stop towerism in government because it's my thinking this 45 president is the only thing that did it in other words un-clogging them so we now see there are so many other outsiders falling that may have been put in the light for the people to see and stop from stealing and doing the wrong thing in the government to the government or outside of the government now that is the silver lining of the storm that the no. 45 brought to the table.

As of 8-23-18 I can't say what will happen now that no. 45 has gone left of the center line of his past and the future that are colliding. I am wholeheartedly sure we do not need to take this set up of any man's problems, personal or otherwise in to our live and if he get four more that is what will happen. This is up to use do we have enough sense to not do that? I think we do we as a people are not that blind foolish or crazy.

Do I want to add the worldly perspective?

If I am on target with the reality that the world is in need the domino affect will take place and kick in so that other countries can become aware of the ungodly people that are in both the government and private businesses that have towerism running things that are not in a healthy way for the layman because of the immoral way they do the things they do. That is my personal opinion. This is a spiritual doctrine that is being released to bless the world.

To take things and put them on another level, do we want to place another state of problem's in our own pathway because we feel guilty about some thing we done or are doing.

That is only because we have been a hellafied nation to a certain measure. We have destroyed many lives inside and outside the country. Sometimes we reap what we sow but we do not have to sow anything worse than what is being done and smeared in our faces.

The actions that may one day reflect on our being a bully in the past that we don't want to rock the boat about that this is a sign.

At the time this was typed we looked at some facts. Lots of the country was on fire at the time I wrote this

in a sense because of the presence of places it is
burning down. This is a sign and warning to the
people that if we had anymore of this country burning
it would be hard to stop it because we wouldn't have
enough resources and it would be so devastating.
This is what Trump is a fire out of control just like the
out of control fires that are burning in our country now.

Trump needs to be doused with a cool drink of reality
and put out before he gets a chance to do anymore
damage and sending any more flames that are
burning throughout the world. We have put enough
garbage into the atmosphere and on the planet and
now we are paying for it. It is time to recognize this
metaphor and stop the madness because if we put up
with enough hellish movement it will come back in
different ways.

Something about the Author

I have been in so much pain lately in my life for the
last 25-30 years because of the social pains of what
could be added to the GPTSD. It propelled me to
write more to help people on a spiritual level to help
myself. The pain came from not being able to help
people so I write. Now can I look forward to some
peace within myself? I believe so and the way I will
know this is the world has more of it.

What I do helps me out of a writer's quandary that I
have found myself in over one half of my life. I have
worked through the quandary in order for me to
escape the isms that I am fortunate to be free of.

The book is a guide to stop and clean up the controversy about the newly elected president. It is a way to help stop hatred of people toward one another along with the fact to show a new light that can help the government become a better place and the people be more able to get along and get things done.

This book will help people who are not happy about the way the government has been running and or the new president to grow up a lot more in the right ways plus give spiritual enlightenment to anyone who may need to add more faith and hope to their life with the blessings of the Lord to free them from GPTSD.

With the power of knowing how to weather any kind of political storm over the next few years; knowing the more you know about something the less you fear.

So we are in the present when you know it is inclusion and not division that gets you in the right state of mind with others.

Through this therapy that the Lord has put in place for the country is of an existence of a presence that can complete a state of thought that belongs to everyone who has the will to learn of spiritual development on somewhat of an old presence that has described itself in a way that looks out of the way made to see a new kind of light In it.

The components for growth that are revealed in this book give the way out of no way that classified itself in a category that brings a peace to fix some of the broken love we as a people didn't know as much

about as we needed to because of our distraction of
innovation that got us lost out of our sight of the way a
heart can escape from its pain that we need not share.
This has harmed some people where their pain gives
them an escape from reality that they can grow out
and away from.

For me it doesn't feel good to know people harming
people does exist. That is why this book help so it can
show a way to change to make new an escape plan
from it to seek out the blind spot in one's self that may
need to be unveiled to show a way out of a hunger
with a meal to put on the table of life. That is what this
may do for the people.

There is a saying that you can't miss anything you
never had. That is so untrue because if you miss out
on different levels of love you may miss your own
presence of self out of reality and it isn't a joke.

Nevertheless it does Make Sense

As adults, we should never play cat and mouse
games with each other no matter whose side you are
on. If we live in the USA we can stand together.

We are preparing a way today for tomorrow's
presence of self to be able to weather any storm
properly.

People shouldn't let mankind stress their endurance
to a limit where it or they snap because the will in
one's self has a divine order that it shares in spirit to
protect it from the fact of conceding to foolishness. It

is time to put your will up where it belongs in the
safety of the Lord; this does help.

Without proper guidance too many children get stuck
on a fairy tale wishing well lifestyle. That causes them
problems throughout their life that leaves them open
to the void-noid numb-dumb lame-duck sin-drone for
danger to enter; this must stop. There may have been
all age limit left out of this wisdom so let's know we
are never too late or old to learn.

The Turning Point

To have a great society you must
teach a higher volume of wisdom

We can stop living in somewhat of a false sense of
security whereby the government owns people. The
people now need to learn how to own the government!
I have learned that trying to change the pathway of
our country takes a greater love than we have been
sharing. Therefore, put your love to work for all
mankind to add unquenchable hope.

The Fact is or Remains

Who cares about someone who is standing on their
own convictions when they are wrong? Do not be
jaded about learning from it. It is to see the truth and
know it but not admit to it. It is not the more things
change the more things remain the same unless you
are learning from them.

The symptoms and the cure

This is self-prejudice caused by the lack of wisdom that people have who thinks they can misconstrue the truth. People who don't want to earn the truth in their life right now have it. The curse of the diversity of a culture does not know how to not include skin color in their practice of thinking that is one of a puzzle of pain to some but not to all.

To Begin 2018-2020

The bottom and top line to it is that we don't have to put ourselves into a perpendicular reality that has appeared and should not phase us as Americans and only God knows the level of our personal presence in the governing of our lives.

This may be a part of the peoples who are caught between the cataclysms in their mind to pray for. This is the beginning of a new kind of quantum leap that may land you in a heavenly state of mind if you are one?

This may be one of the best ways at this time in history for people to lay claim to their spiritual equity that they were born with, without going through some kind of hellish situation. To bless the Lord please take whatever you need out to promote this much needed book.

We are ready for the big news

Hello again and thank you for your time

There is a silver lining behind the voting in the 45th president and there is the storm behind it also. Again, thanks to you we see that silver lining and that is what helps us make it through the storm.

He also gave one of the greatest, if not the greatest, example of a towerist to the American people and the world. It is a two-fold way to be proud of him and not at the same time.

This is not a part of the start
but it is a part of the finish line!

Now what we can learn from this can be a life-saving process of growth that can stop us from letting people take advantage of others. The big picture is the whole world can benefit from what is learned from this wisdom.

About the author

The level of trauma that I went through in my life and having no one there on somewhat of a one on one basis put me through a kind of living hell. The Lord kept me company thanks to the Holy Spirit and the seeds that was planted by my mother and father also my family, friends, preachers and teachers in ministry.

This writing is for all Americans of every ethnicity: a way to help keep and increase our freedom. A way to love all who make it up to behold.

Again welcome to a new level of stability

There is a real silver lining in the 45th president, even though I did not vote for him

Will he be someone who will stay stuck in a tower and furthermore, keep the trap set for his family more so his sons in towerism? The jury is out.

Will he step up for the people who love him and not let them take one more negative blow because he refused to not just go out of the White House like a champ? What will be the verdict? Can he at least go out like a champ?

It is time to stop living in the fight that stinks. It is time to learn about the stink before you fight reality. Don't be stuck like chuck.

Advice

Fool me once shame on you. Fool me twice shame on me. Don't shame yourself for anyone. It isn't that serious. If we had a big blunder come in our lifetime it is not keep wondering in and with the incomplete idea it can change things and make things better overall. It can't so don't get stuck on the superficial.

The information in the book talks about the government in Washington, DC, but the issue is in all small and large towns and cities in the USA and we need to look out for anyone with a toweristic agenda they want to use on the people and put a stop to it.

Now what one of the best thing we can do is not let anymore towerists in government right now. It is critical to add a kind of prevention factor to and in our homeland.

I would like you to know your true patriotism in life that leads you to do good. This process is an investment in the kingdom building. It is for the life-saving advancement of people in order to give them more self-help and to enhance their spiritual skills which give more of the ability to receive communion with the Lord.

This is one of the most vital attributes any human can have and without it you may find yourself in a precarious situation.

M-N

The investment of your leaning you make is a part of your personal gift to what you have been made steward over that the Lord has blessed you with. It is put also on your account in heaven and the return that is gives is no match for what God can give you so always give to other always.

A Solution

This is a way to not allow civil disobedience into the content of the way we live and show each other love to understand the power within and maintain its control.

To the people

The greatest asset you can get with this tool is it puts you in touch with common sense. Nothing more, nothing less and that isn't a bad deal.

To me

I have fought a better than good fight. It is time to stop the fight and get ready for the flying to be done.

S-N

How does this grab you if we don't cause anymore disruption in the country because of what no. 45 has done we may be looking at the scale being good and close to an equal balance; or is it a steal?

What is really going on is the fact that this is not just a book but it is a way of developing the expansion and growth of life. It is like a basic garden that has principles that have to be maintained: the cultivating of it, the de-weeding of it and also letting the water that comes from your love run out of you because of your sweat equity because of the perception that one puts into this, as well as not knowing or knowing how to not eat a poisonous fruit.

You could say this book is like a present day mirage of the Garden of Eden as a lot of other of my writings are that people can utilize the wisdom and make sure they pass it on so that others may have a way to naturally develop themselves without causing extra chaos, confusion and harm to others. This is a spiritual skills garden where you can grow into the body of Christ in a polite and very generous mannerism to show that you care and you want to be cared for without fear.

Some would say this is today's foresight to live by for the tomorrows in our society.

Look up the answer is here

This is a part of the big picture to open your heart

The main reason for this developmental information is to start to defeat and deflate the purpose of becoming negative in protests and rallies. The government PSTD builds up in individuals. When it comes time for the voting process to take place is when it exposes itself and explodes in anger and violence and that is why we are deflating it now with the information that is out so by the time the election gets here and the other necessary things involving gatherings it will be a peaceful venture instead of a violent one thanks to God's intervention.

The books will help end political wars as well as help end spiritual wars in America. That will help stop the division between people which has two ways to create and/or cause them in major ways, one is religion, the other is political disagreements.

Some other reading material may be Paul Dunbar's common ground. Also look in the Bible for some other information you can use. Do this for yourself because we get weary sometimes but even when Jesus got weary sometimes he would get in a boat alone and away from people to not be disturbed. You have heard the story of some things that happened when he was there.

Rest on his word that we all can use.

This is a part of the bringing together of like minded and non-like minded people so we can all take a stand for peace regardless to our diversity of interests.

I hope my level of engaging and promoting the dialogue is to everyone's likeness even though they may not totally agree.

The reading I think would be enjoyable would be a book by Burke, a new book about Lincoln.

How many times do we need to re-invent ourselves? It is because of societal issues that we must take on that have created a default in a positive level of energy. We have to remove the negativity from it and reinvent it in a positive way as many times as needed. This is another way of reinventing the motions that have been in this part of living from the beginning of mankind and will be forever.

Is this a good news moment?

Could this information become one of the ways through the factor that this is the ram by way of bro. bush and the writing he does?

I hope this is the right annunciation that has put together the right narrative to connect with you. Without connection it is futile.

What it is all about

You are not an enemy you are only an adversary with a different objective. We can compromise and do great things. We can use the wisdom we have been blessed with to multiply our ability to stay peaceful.

The good part about it is there are so many people hating on Trump and I could be one of them but the Lord said love your enemy and if you feel that way because he is doing things contrary to the way things should be done you should love your enemy. This is a perfect example of what love can do when you project loveoutame to others. This is what I am projecting to him and anyone else who feels differently than I feel and/or think.

It may sound a little outlandish but if we change government at this time in history we change the world for all mankind.

If you still believe in him then believe that he will do the right thing. Pray and believe and pray for freedom from government rule. Until we get this out of the way we will still be in a disarray because of bureaucratic nonsense and attitudes of towerism.

We have a duty to help him be in a position to win as a politician and commander in chief. That is what towerists do, they take advantage of things. If he feels that is what the majority wants him to do he will. The time is now to take advantage of this opportunity.

This could be one of the best things we could help no. 45 do for the government and also bringing his family from under the bondage he has been under as a towerist.

It is time to cause them not to be able to undermine the people. We can override and veto their ability to take the votes from the majority. It is a timely thing now and we can do it.

About the electoral college

He can submit the pass or make an executive order or decision to conquer this negative trait of government that has stood in the way of progress because of towerists that are around the country running it. At one time it may have been a good policy but now it is outdated.

Now may be the best time ever to convince the president if we send him enough kites, fliers, letters, emails to put forth a bill in Congress to end the process of the electoral vote, especially if he thinks he will get the popular vote. If he feels that he is that powerful and strong with the people then he won't mind but if enough people give him the thought and that option we can see how things go. We can take the most positive thing we can and make it a different kind of stand in the White House because we can help him and he can help himself.

This is revelation time not revolution time

Now that you understand your vote has caused a great awakening, what we need to do now is not go into a great migration or in other words let's keep things moving forward and we do not need a violent state of being if he loses or wins. We must go into a greater level of the loveoutame presence in life.

To complete this task we must let everyone know that we are living in the now change generation or the change things now generation. This is what is going on from now on and we will be living there for the rest of our lives and throughout eternity as the people of the body of Christ on earth living in a now change generation for the betterment of humanity. Amen and hallelujah for the fellowship.

Could it be that we need the Trump to trump the towers regardless to what has been going on or taking place since he has been in office? I think it is a great possibility that we needed that trump card to make everything else fold as it has been doing so let's rebuild and re-stack the deck.

Now is it such thing as people being afraid of being in control of the government because they had no understanding of what was really going on and was kept in the dark. Now that all the light has come into the vision you have the ability to use this foresight to get out of the unsecured daylight that the government itself has not even understood that it ruled and the people who ruled it gave notice to stay in the darkness so they could stay in the height of the power of the towers. The towers are now falling and it is up

to us to keep the domino affect going so that the
world can be a better place.

The workings of God is sometimes mysterious.
Is this one of those times?

Can this be a part of the domino affect that takes
down the towers of the electoral colleges to? I think
so. Make it so people because it is up to you can this
be the right time to change this!

That is why it is good to be able to comprehend these
things about the silver lining and everything involved
may be one of the biggest opportunities to create the
downfall and taking down of many towers that have
been in control of the electoral college voting system
so that the majority will be the one to determine the
next president. The electoral college voting system
can now be defeated. It is time for it to go.

If anyone wants to look at the statement I just made in
a different way that is their prerogative. The fact of the
matter is I am not a person who doesn't wants to feel
uncomfortable so I don't want anyone else to feel
uncomfortable no matter what I am expressing in
trying to bring about change to make humanity better.

I do not want to pass judgment on anyone but the real
estate that one carries in their heart that has been
developed in heaven will be the real estate that one
will stay on when they get there. The priceless things
of our world are not priceless because of their
worthlessness. For the towerists there will be very
little real estate compared to those who have learned

to make great gains by blessing others with the little they have.

Can we say that this process had to become a state of reality in order to shake the foundations of the presence of mankind to his own shortcomings and his own negative develop? I think so and I think we all need to take a pause in order for us to prevent abuse by using this self-esteem as insight to our future.

Maybe this is a challenge but the fact is Trump became USA's 45th president. The challenge is to see whether or not the people can adapt to extreme changes in the way they perceive things in the development of putting together a presence of new truth from old mistakes that took place in history that possibility could have been prevented.

The process of starting now in an element of understanding and growth and accepting what has taken place and moving forward is a challenge that we must now make if we are to make any kind of developmental growth as a nation of people.

Don't mind me calling our president Uncle Slam. It is time to consider getting a Colonel Sam in there. Then we may see more positive actions from the leader of this country.

To help understand the grand growth of this getting on a new reality and beat. That is why I wrote the book to help soldiers who commit suicide, I consider our Uncle Sam or Uncle Slam who needs to become Colonel Sam and change this level of thinking and acting in the eyes of God and not looking at what man has to say all the time because some of it doesn't make sense.

Who can join in and say

I will not let it project this level of negativity in my existence regardless to the fact that it is the government because it is not the godliness that it gives out as it should. No longer will I see the government as an undeveloped unrecognized threat that it is to the country we live in. we thank God for this new lighthouse that comes above the White House in reality.

The black is out in the right house

You have now been de-cloaked as a body of misunderstanding and misdetermination and unknown and unwittingly developing negativity.

We can tell the government you can not raise any more hell in me that comes from the dark side of the Satanic level of man-made disasters.

To the towerists

In other words, you are super-greedy in your lifestyles. Now you will have to face retribution later.

That doesn't mean you won't make it into heaven it only says your account is being depleted. That is going to be a reality that you will live in throughout eternity. If you don't like it remember that you can change it. If you don't it still beats being in hell.

In other words some people think they have their heads so far into the Lord's they think their own butts don't stink. But they need to learn how to but out of lots of stuff that is between individuals and the Lord. Instead they try to run and govern the lives of others making them think they have a greater power than they have. It really only lessens their power of being human in the eyesight of God. Believe it and retreat instead of thinking you are in a class of high and mighty people. You may be in a matchbox in heaven looking at those sitting in mansions.

There is one problem lots of people have: they are too busy trying to stick their noses up the Lord's butt. The Lord doesn't have a butt for you to stick your nose in. The reason I say this is because they try to act like they are running a part of his business. They need to come back down to earth. If they want to be up someone's butt smell their own butts because that is where the stink is. Please excuse my bad language.

To stop that process of good people going to hell, it takes one thing: allow the Lord to save your soul so you don't end up one of those good people who go to hell.

Time can still be on our side don't blow it!

To anyone who is interested in what I am doing with the assistance of my longest somewhat living friend, my pen. I have been, as it has been, a consistent and even though it has given me a few minutes of fame here and there, it is always saying it is not about you. What it is saying is about what others can get out of it.

I am pursuing the fact of how many more days, weeks and/or years it will take before a multitude of people discover what they may be in need of within the writings I do that is inspired by the Holy Spirit.

An inner look at me. Did I get lost out in the wilderness intentionally to teach myself a lesson or was it my destination to be lost out of the main stream of society to protect myself and my work? I think both. Not a joke it is a truth I can live with even though it is not my greatest truth.

A letter to all

To the public at large: I am a piece of the body of Christ. I have been called to develop a way to help the country survive and move forward in this unseen crisis that can become more well known. If it is not stopped to help to do this I have completed a taste of the book the silver lining to further our health and wellness in a united way.

The process is to expose the 45th president in a way that shows his silver lining that everyone has. Additionally, there is the cloud he is in that creates rainstorms and lightning that can lead to darkness for people who are already less fortunate in ways that the Lord has appointed us to protect in ways that have lots to do with any kind of election.

To stop the unreasonable people who want to govern the land that we are to be stewards over as disciples of the Lord no matter what title you have: preacher, teacher, butcher, baker, candlestick maker. Here is the blessings that we have been waiting on to help change the world with elections at this time, none too small, none too large. The time is here to heed the calling the Lord has for you no one is exempt who can vote!

To make it known all I want to do is include my part of love that the Lord gave me to share as I did at the RNC/DNC as in the book subtitled The 24th helper. There were 23 other agencies there and I made up the 24th who was sent by the Lord. Thank God he sent me because I was the one who stopped a possible riot at the RNC in downtown Cleveland, Ohio at the time it was going on.

Who knows what is next to do that help mankind and the body of Christ. This process of work I have been a part of in the past gave insight to the people in this nation. I would consider it an honor and privilege to add even more to be apart of sharing in the blessings with the people of America.

I will also be looking forward to being wherever the next RNC/DNC convention to lend a hand to the Lord and work to keep the love in front with peace to be shared with all. It can be handled like a kind of MardiGras in the presence of the Lord so the devil can pass us by.

It is an all hands on deck to become a shoulder in the process of voting because if you do not vote you are still voting for someone and that may be the wrong one.

To help show the way back to the right state of growth a book titled: *The Comeback of America* which is due to be released by the first of the year 2019. this will help add reverence to the other books that can help make life better for people. It could be subtitled: how to do that thing by using what is in the love that we produce out of the wisdom we have to show others so there is created no fuss or must if we agree by adding it together and doing what is right.

I recommend you read the book titled *Fear* by Bob Woodward. It might help people get a greater understanding of why I wrote *Fixing what is Broken in America by Stopping Towerism* and *Calm During the Storm* along with *Ending Political Wars in America*. Then most of all to put the icing on the cake *The Recovery of the U.S. Government/The Power of Knowing "No," No. 2* when it is done. There is even more information at BTHPM for anyone who is going into politics.

To the readers: we all are challenged in life and it is a trial period. We have to pick our self up and we look for help this I offer is help then it is family and friends and faith that also steps in to give the extra hand.

We have to support ourselves in ways as if it is not what you can do for us but what we can do for ourselves.

If you are not one help stop someone from being like a lamb being led to slaughter.

This is a healthy adult way to keep growing up and maturing with an understanding of how to share the love and stop the hating on others

So many die from abuse take this insight

Helping to Stop Bullies' Bullets This may be out of the way talk but I can consider the book Time to stop the abuse, etc to prevent harm. As It is a kind of forerunner to this book somewhat as the few other books about the government are too or is this vice-versa.

This can be considered a new presence daylight if you are one who have consider that the government has left you out into a state of darkness. With faith this can be like an eternal spring that pops up out of a desert in a desire and not like a wishing well that casts a futile spell.

This is a good sign from the Lord

The moral of the information is we all have silver linings. We shouldn't allow ourselves to inflate this part of us in ways that supersede the morals that we need to maintain, which could be looked at as the art of the deals with people.

Some people get so lost in their own lining they get tripped up and harm others because of selfish center levels of blindness that the prince of darkness has a way of placing on them. It causes others to feel the unrighteousness they have and somewhat lived by. This as a sickness of an ungodly spiritual kind that makes them feel entitled to go through life with it. If they have been caught in traps of towerism and they are not well to do with money they get lost out of touch with themselves and others; how unfortunate.

This may be something that pushes some people into sin. They need to know that freedom is available thanks to the willpower the Lord shares with us.

Ungodly news

It is like some of the catholic got hook on there own silver lining in the wrong ways that also made them create a cover up for the perverseness they had in the clergy.

Now the silver lining is supposed to be a better than good thing but it to can carry a bad part to it if someone thinks too highly of themselves as a towerist or some of the people who serve God and act like public servants. This is not new it is just brought forth in a way that the Lord has commissioned.

A forewarning from the Lord

Now there is one thing about the silver lining it will find a way to tell or snitch on it self if you are fortunate and if not the Lord will deal with you later and that may be unfortunate. I also think this maybe some kind of out word warning to be know by man kind that came from up high.

Being that way will or can amount to a waste of life that thinks it is living. No one will give a damn about you feeding of your misuse of your own silver lining long after you are gone no one at all so change it. God has show you or can, a way to use it the right way to not live in it by yourself to a certain measure without rhyme or a very good reason forever.

To know that the silver lining is a part of our stepping stone to get us to a higher level of love in life as the loveoutame that leads up to greater love. At the same time to get locked up in self from a kind of craziness is the thing that harms people to also harm others in adverse ways.

This is a plague that came down through Egypt and Rome that was created by the Pharisees, Sadducee and Pharaoh who built up temples and towers to create their own eternity before the Lord came and it is still a kind of plague on the earth that some people have that have a hard time giving there time and heart and mind to the Lord that doesn't have an ailing bone in them but are lost in their own silver lining. They were sick toweristic and perverted people like those who lived in Basra in ancient times, who affected some of the catholic clergy.

Now ask the Lord to free you from your own silver lining and watch the new feelings that come over you. In Jesus' name.

Too much zealousness can have a slightly negative connotation and people are sometimes described as overzealous. This is a part of being a towerist you can stop if you see it in you. The change of zest to zeal is needed because every little bit helps to grow out of a state of ungodliness and we should be giving thanks for it.

This new motivation it helps give you
the desire to not disappoint yourself

Part of the advice I give is:
Do not take your silver lining as a joke

We can learn to stop the zealousness from going up into a state of being egotistic that will dominate to present of the conscious state of the will if it doesn't know it is under attack in darkness that catches people off guard to harm them as also when you harm someone else you may be harming one's self even more.

Can this be the time that we are allowed to ask the Lord to remove the silver lining sin-drome from the face of the earth and the body of the spirit of the people? Is it a dimension of presence that causes individuals to have this that have created the gold and silver that the Egyptians used to wear to garnish themselves with so that once they died the spirit that left them was tainted with to a certain measure. After they got back into the heavens the spirit or wherever it went that was sacred that was rejuvenated with possibly another spirit to create more spirits to return to the earth than may be the newborns receive this? This is something we may never know but if it has become a part of the spiritual DNA that has basically saturated throughout the history of people then can and is it time for us to ask the Lord to remove this DNA defection of the spirit and cleanse it because if it has to be cleansed of demons. It can be cleansed of sin-dromes such as the silver lining sin-drome.

The uncanny or somewhat crazy part of it is I had this silver-lining sin-drome myself at one time and thank God for my breakthrough. Now I intend on helping others breakthrough also and come out of that because it is a curse of the forefathers that can be passed along to this generation to come and it needs not be in Jesus' name.

Taking it even further, did the Indians as they were putting on their war paint and also African tribes saturate within their spirit the substance of the earth that gave a bondage to it that may have been developed in an unhealthy way throughout the history of people. We also may never know why the gold and silver was placed upon those Egyptian Pharaohs and scribes and Sadducee and Pharisees.

Even the nation of people who had blood rituals who painted blood on their body and even drank it into their spirits, it is real and did affect the DNA of the spirit as the other parts of the presence that have been presented.

If we are a melting pot we see where we transferred all kinds of dilemmas and demonic presences of possible existences to the growth of mankind. Therefore, we have to know these things in order to protect future generations. What I am trying to convey is don't get lost get found in the ways you live and grow.

Could one of our greatest challenges be to eliminate the darkness from our silver lining and protect it from any other influences that it can have? Or should we proceed to create self war that makes people want to share it outside of themselves. That is what we are helping to fix now.

Where do I think the basis of the silver lining is? I think it is in the eternal spiritual DNA that makes up the heavenly hosts that we have in us as a part of Jesus Christ that can be affected by certain things due to the fact that we still are in the earthly realm and until we understand how to believe in the free will of God we are susceptible to become entangled within that space and place that we now identify with. We now can do something about it in more than one way to protect the life that we have.

The greatest part of the work I am doing is I cannot mess it up. I cannot confuse it or deliver it in the wrong mannerism because of a part of God's will that resides in me.

Believe it and receive it

It is yours and it has been paid for by the Lord and now he is presenting it to you in this generation at this point in time.

The most ironic thing you may have heard is the silver lining can be one of the greatest and most important attributes that we have as humans to give us a zeal of motivation that cannot be compared to anything else but at the same time when it runs into a wrong kind of build up that allows Satan's dirt devil sin-drome to enter because of being human and not having enough spiritual skills this stops the flow of the goodness of it, it is not like anything else. It can turn into gray matter that is in the metabolism that causes dysfunction in the brain and is also morally affected by being spiritually unbalanced. It needs to be put into a new state of existence and realm because it has not received the right nourishment.

Discovering a problem is the first step to a cure. Now that we have discovered it and have ways of understanding why it became that way because of Satan and his demonic process of pushing people into levels of void-noid and numb-dumb because they are not spiritually equipped and need to enhance their spiritual skills so they are not able to be brought down and causes problems.

As I said, we have now grown to a new understanding of thinking that is like a new discovery of how we can fix the DNA of mankind to create better lives for ourselves and others.

Have you ever heard the saying "brother gonna work it out?" well, disciples are going to work it out and that is what is being done. It has been a process of discovery from a sky chief disciple or sapphire blue blooded disciple.

What can you discover once your completion in the spiritual development of skills?

The ability to do the greater things that you were meant to do in the first place without fear. As far as me I have been there in ways I now understand as never before with the skills.

If I don't lead the way to show others how we can discover and conquer old territories to make new territories then why am I talking about or writing about it if I can't get in a mighty blow for justice such as David did with Goliath? There are so many Davids out here that need to be pointed in the right direction to take out negativity. Basically we should be taken out of self first.

The reason why the Lord gives you the grace and mercy of having spiritual endowment on a humbling level is developed through the presence of spiritual skills. They protect you from the misuse of the silver lining that you were born into as an inheritance from Jesus.

How many other countries in the world
can benefit with information such as this?

To all who help others see and hear:

From Bro. Bush, I am requesting your attention about a matter that may be on your agenda as steps to increase the work we can do for the body of Christ.

The point is as a hand in the body I have increased the personal anointing I was given to a level of 40 plus books to enhance the or a fulfillment in our society to become good or great in the loveoutame state of growth. It is not my intent to stop the presence of what you can do to help you do more on all states of the matters we are facing who works within the body of Christ.

The bottom line is we can share a greater level of truth that will increase the power we are to use as a tool. I have a few good ideas I hope you will look into that will fill in some of the blanks that a multitude of may people have.

I am planning to introduce even more of the writing the Holy Spirit has me doing. There are a series of books that can increase the love we share but the way that was chosen for me has put me in line with the needs of the country at large. As a fact, there are a few of the books I have to show some people out of a kind of darkness they may be in need of.

The perfect example of someone with towerism is the current president and one of the book offers a trumpectomy to stop trumpitis that also helps people get free that show more hope to and for our country.

This is in line for some that may be somewhat on the edge but to take it one step further, they can get a book _Calm During the Storm_. But we can step up so to be able to understand the 45th president's silver lining. I mean the son came into the way of darkness as need be.

The fact that we all have silver linings is not to be a mystery but the imperfection that can surround it may be harmful for some. That is what this new book does. It can take people to a place of lifting a veil of darkness and fear. It reveals the way the silver lining shows up in the 45th president.

Furthermore, it delivers people out of the clouds' nests with the storms in them. It will also bring the light that is needed and not the lightning that strikes some people because of some of the leadership in government that knows not what they are doing or don't care. Therefore, the sight for the blind can be gained as a start along with the wisdom.

This new book and others will be official crises relief centers that teaches to reflect the spelling out GPTSD off of them. It is what has affected millions throughout the years and has caused chaos radioing I need not say more. I will say from the way the Lord had me present _The Devil Passed Me By_; that is another book I have authored with the guidance of the Holy Spirit. It stopped what could have been a major problem at the RNC in Cleveland.

This is not a phony element. It is as if we are on trial as the body of Christ and the fake ideas have separated themselves from what God said is real as the silver lining. So many clergy are under fire to stop their madness as was in the Catholic community.

Learn to see what may be a way to promote the work I am doing if you have it in your heart. Go to the website to be prepared to do the right thing in the upcoming elections. If you think it is right what is being done at Bound to Heaven Publishing/Ministries. Please don't pass me by I have a need to be on what platform the Lord has opened up the doors which keep me humble.

See me as the man of God I am and the time has come for the ram that has been tempered by still called Bro. Bush to bring this state of loveoutame to the nation of the body to increase what the Lord establish in the heavens that he wants the multitudes to know.

On the up and up

To stop a part of Satan's dieconomie

To be know one of the latest book to be release in 2018 titled *Help to Stop Bullies' Bullets*, subtitled, Ending a part of Satan's Dieconomie of Killing.

This is a part of the introduction of the tasks the master has call me to. Can you help? The one way is to invite you to promote one or more of the book I have along with the measure of getting the kind of messages that the Lord may want you to have.

Keep in mind

The best thing in life comes from the use of power and to know one of the number one thing that gives us that is truth. Therefore, to accept it is the wisdom of it all because there are some who are hung up on not wanting to accept the truth because they will see themselves wrong. That is what you may not want to face that is why to close your eyes and say Lord protect me from myself and weakness of not accepting the truth so I will know what or the truth is my heart's desire.

We all can help fix it

This gives two labels for one

We have a world of galayif's people that is anyone who can learn to be a conqueror who have a lazy gall of if I do what I should do what might happen to me. They have too much influence on failing and fear. That needs to be eliminated from their conscious or subconscious. Turn the galayif's into the right kind of Goliath. There is a time for a new kind of therapy from the Lord. There is no better day for it than today. Now who said words aren't to have fun with is wrong, even at the serious times in life!

To add it all up the wisdom can be supplied to your life but if it isn't made from love it is not everlasting so it can be an unfulfilled kind of wisdom that needs more to its presence because a piece of knowledge can keep you hanging and if you hang on to something (or someone) that is not full you might fall. So get it all with no half stepping.

The books are about the USA's plan to outweighs and increase our protecting ourselves from ourselves and any foreigners who want to harm us. This understanding may be a way to exit the house within, that has developed negative silver linings, and start fresh.

The politicians' job is to protect the people of the land from any storm on land, air or sea. But this wisdom can help get them out of a kind of satanic limbo presence to move them forward with the Lord.

It is time we end having a world with so many galayif's people (anyone who came to be a gouch). That is someone with the potential to be Goliath in a good way that has things backward with there thinking.

What makes things kind of bad and sad is the GPTSD is in today yesterday and tomorrow's time that haunts and hurts and affects people and it also has the ability to blow up with the next political uprising to damage the people and makes a kind of hell or all kinds of hell rain down on America.

Take off the blinders like a horse racing

This is the help for people who get tied into much of their mental well being at times instead of their spiritual health.

S-N

It is time to stop being stuck like chuck in the muck and believing in luck.

I would like everybody to think of the book as one big aspirin for the world to give relief from trumpitis.

To a sometimes undetermined level there is common sense missing to an unknown space that comes out in towerism that may not have a great degree of moral balance.

This can be a life starter

It is time to change the name of your title if you are a towerist of any kind start thinking of yourself as a positive influence. This kind of person is, or stands for, a vigilante justice.

If anyone wants to know why I write so much about politicians it is to show people the sickness and madness of the demonic construction that is a part of it to watch out for. I do this to give the presence of people to be able to see the nobility of a good character or not, with a Godly insight that only God can give someone. But even so it can help someone help self.

You can take anything in life and make a reason for it to be right or wrong. But the true measure comes when you defeat the wrong with right.

Now let's take the prolific surrounding the silver lining. It could be as unique because it has been developed into a circular pattern as if someone was wearing it as a halo or it could be something that encompasses the spiritual body in a way that circles it and encompasses the heart. You never want it to get out of order and fall into a dimension where it is down at the bottom where it is dirtied with the crap in the mental process of thinking.

Now we can take things and keep them in the proper perspective by imagining that people are developing halos and have their spirit guides that really gives spiritual skills even those who have not been taught anything but they still catch on to be made aware, it is as simple as that.

The silver lining could be subtitled humpty dumpty on the tower wall. Will he fall if he can't build his wall and crack his bulb so all his yoke will spill all over the place making us out of even a greater joke.

It is already shown that those who sit next to him on the wall on the tower so many have fallen down because of his acting a clown. Who will be next? Will the country take a fall because of this big, childish egg head sitting on the wall?

I am not the best writer by no means, but I do give some of the best light on matters that count. Also, I bring the truth to grow better with something that can led people out of troubles.

To be standing in the exact spot and coordinate things to be in the right time frame to prevent a run in is only the way it was meant to be.

We are ending unknown wars
that can't be seen but can be felt

Now can the way we have been handling the
traumatosed people and especially those with the
government GPTSD that has been put on people. We
have a way out from under it so let's use it.

Taking note: there are some races that we can get in
where the fun is in the running and not in just winning.
Don't figure just get in it for the run. In other words,
you can just want to participate regardless to win, lose
or draw it is fun to just run sometimes.

Good will

It is just a thought but I believe that Senator John
McCain parting help to end a great deal of the now
and future political wars and spiritual wars this country
has and was facing. Additionally, in retrospect to the
senator let's get something done. We can now
because I feel he has left us with a part of his hero or
heroism spirit. I would like to put it in perspective with
his last speech. God has blessed him and his family.

On another pathway

To add even another level of a man baby the space
force process of thinking is a child like issue."

Is this work a kind of testing ground of knowledge?
You will be pleasantly surprised if you try it.

Everyone should never think the majority of goodness is a kind of hokus pokus because real magic is or comes from the growth of love.

One of the best things to learn

As Americans we never want to let another towerist into the government/White House on any level. With the use of this wisdom we can get ahead of this kind of problem and help others.

To go where I don't want to go but I must. The people who have towerism attributes feel privileged and entitled to more than others and feel that other are minute and are not their equal and it is a way of hiding behind prejudices and bigotry.

The way the government has taken over somewhat in other countries throughout the world with towerists interfering and running a part of them that are falling apart it is because of the lack of a Godly vision and without vision a nation will go into turmoil and come apart as some are doing.

The beast called selfish greed takes over and tries to kill love as much as it can and most of the time it is unseen but when it rises up it kills and this must be stopped. We the people in the USA don't want a tip of this kind of iceberg on our doorstep. So join in to help stop it. In the name of our lord and Savior Jesus Christ.

Here is the crazy thing: some people who voted for no. 45 president are so mad at him they want to take it

out on others who didn't vote for him because they
feel they have influenced him to get outlandish. But
this is the furthest from the truth and they may also be
mad at themselves because they feel bad about not
being totally right and can't accept they are at least
one-half right that can be the most important asset to
hold on to. The main problem with this is not forgiving
one's self.

Any name appearing in this book is strictly
unauthorized and no permission was given to use it.

I would like to also take my hat off to Senator John
McCain. I admire him for lots of things but mostly his
integrity.

As I said in one of my previous book, if you are a
towerist you have the trapping of a man baby as
someone who plays flag games.

S-N

Out of everyone I don't know I think Lebron James
and Tiger Woods may agree with what can be learned
out of the book. One of the reasons I say this is I
believe they are not towerists.

Could my writings be considered the opposite of
crime or something that add more time to humanity?

Now what we have is a total mad element of Satan's
planting his seeds of destruction into people. It has
gotten out of control like the individuals who are
towerists who have become molesters. What we have

63

is a reality of taintedness that is still going on in darkness in high places and in the dark state of mind. What does the government have to do with the underdog that wants to do right? They feel like why should they when the so-called leaders are doing what they want to.

Those small towerists who want to be large towerists who are killing, robbing, etc. or trying to mask their problems with drugs or whatever causes them to be in a diverted way of being a pervert or whatever just as the catholic clergy, who have damaged their own silver lining. The main thing is now we can save those who are little towers running around and teach them to not want to destroy their ability so they can be free from their bondage. It causes them to try to get things the easy way instead of working for it. They act like someone who has an excuse to want to get ahead the wrong way when basically they need to live with to less to gain more in order for them to begin their spiritual quest of spiritual skills development. That is the top, middle and bottom line to issues that we have that can be fixed. I believe some people would rather make a so-called deal with the Lord.

I would like you to think of me as just a part of the body of Christ. Now the Lord is extending his arms out to those who can touch his hand in their fellow man with the loveoutame he is presenting in a way to not allow the tombs and dooms of time that has ravaged so many people's minds to continue to corrupt and disrupt the lives of people who need to know freedom in a mannerism they have never known before. That is what is being presented to all. At the end of the day, we only have his words to rely on the ways he has developed them to present to us.

I am doing the best I can to make sure you get a full measure of wisdom on your plate by the time you are finished and are edified by the messages I am presenting to free those who are lame, cripple or crazy. I have been all of them at one time so I can't deny anyone what I have been given because it was given to me by the Lord to share with others so they can have the same freedom and be powerful in their right to pursue the joy, happiness and careers towards their own personal glory and the reunification of them with the body of Christ. There have been too many separated and lost and falling into the sea of fire which is now being extinguished with the water that douses it and puts it out.

It is time to become deradicalized. There is no need to have the radicalized nature that has the creepy crawly within that is the beast of the field in a way that may be individuals in high places or individuals who have no tower or even a place. It is time to refrain from that illusive demonic presence of existence that draws out the negative presence of something that you were not meant to become a part of or share in with the way you present yourself on a conscious level and a spiritual level and a moral level. This is time for deradicalization so that the newfound production of the loveoutame can be developed to present the wholeness and wellness and fullness of what we are to be as Christians or good people in general. These are the facts that have now been presented so we can begin to redefine what being a human is in a multitude of people who have lost their way to humanism and have become humanimalistic in their development. They may have the riches or wealth or nothing at all. It has affected individuals on all levels. Now the change has come to fruition and we can accept it because we understand it wholeheartedly.

To aid with your therapy keep in mind at all times the Lord's prayer especially the part about leading me not into temptation but deliver me from evil for thine is the kingdom and the power and the glory forever and ever Amen. Do not hesitate once a negative thought comes into your head about harming someone. Say get behind me Satan and furthermore you are dismissed and you are to disappear forever from my inner silver lining so that I never become a part of your dieconomie harming anyone. Focus on that if you ever feel those unworthy thoughts of the presence of Satan because he has no power over you but you have power over him in Jesus' name.

Let's take it home and home is where the heart is. We have a new presence of the body of Christ and a developmental process of not only restructuring and re-educating some of the principles that we have been unaware of that exists but taking the growth within the loveoutame that reflects in the mirror the smartoutame process that is like two towers standing together that we can align ourselves with enough teaching and wisdom to go between them and develop a stairway to heaven but not in the sense as those individuals collectively did in building the Tower of Babel when they wanted to build a stairway to heaven. These factors alone can be developed in one's heart and give them a presence of a place to share their experience with others sharing their gifts from the Lord so they can multiply them and create the works of the Lord and not be surprised to be presented with a miracle or two in life to share in the body of Christ to build into the building.

The task of knowing this is one thing and developing it is another. It will require study to be approved. Now I am one like some of other disciple makers that can tell you that you can walk a mile or a thousand miles in my shoes in a present sense of learning.

All you have to do is start reading and excuse me for my mistakes along the way of your travels through the reading material I have been blessed to develop. Sometimes it may not seem easy but if you keep pursuing the development of your discipleship on whatever level, you can accomplish the goal of being someone to share the blessings of the Lord to help the multitude of individuals to become greater sharers of love with each other. Hallelujah to you and yours and amen for all we do within the body of Christ and as individuals.

The sad thing about a towerist is they are really individuals who are wondering around with everything in the world they may want on one level but are basically like someone with no sense of how far lost in the wilderness they are because of being lost in the towerist presence of a fall which they refuse to take back or acknowledge wholeheartedly that the Lord is king and he is in control or they just have a sickness in them they refuse to let go. That is why this freedom bell is now ringing between the loveoutame and the smartoutame process. The higher we reach the more we can ring that freedom bell for those who are lost out in the towerist level whether on the low or high part of the totem pole. Thank God gives us answers to our problems daily and in time and on time if we just listen.

What can be the most disenchanting part of discovering that our towerists have silver linings being human and have a developmental process of the silver lining turned into a fake or faded gray colored cloud. The higher up they go in losing touch with reality of humanity the more the silver lining turns into a gray cloud. They think it is still of a venue that has a touch of wisdom about it and really it is nothing but fading into obscurity for self-denial and also having the sin-drome of someone who is lost in outer space place where it may be an indefinite avenue they cannot walk back down unless they crash, fall or burnout.

It is not a pleasant thing to think about but it is real, the discovery of freedom needs to be placed at their doorstep so they can trip over it to understand their presence and existence. Like they say, good people go to hell too.

We are going to take things to another perspective. For those who are in the towers, if you understand how to go between the loveoutame and the smartoutame process you can learn to come out of the tower to give you a way to freedom but you have to understand that you need to be educated and accept the fact that you may be one of those who may be trapped. It may give a way to stay there.

Using the loveoutame and smartoutame process as others use them as stairways to heaven you can use them as stairways down to an earthly presence of developing your awareness as one who does not want to remain in a wandering state.

The greatest thing about it is those who are there may not know they are there but those who have an idea they may be in a towerist state can at least go through the motion of developing the process of learning and grabbing the wisdom and holding it close to their bosom so they can release the negativity and their heart can start to be right toward humanity as it should be in the eyes of the Lord and in the spirit of themselves.

Winning wars have changed its course in history. It now requires you to walk softly and carry use and share the right set of tools. That way you can not only end it but win it at the same time. The first fight is the one with self to know you are right.

You can basically let someone know there is no need to fight against themselves with the right tools. In order for them to create the necessary obedience in themselves. There have been too many people who had no knowledge of whether they were right or wrong so they kept the fight up. Now it is not necessary because you can give them the right determination and analogy for keeping the peace movement which we should all be one to save as many souls as we can so the Lord can redeem them.

Know this: the little pebble that you throw in a pond may sometimes create a bigger ripple than what you can think of if God has it planned that way.

Maybe the book in the Bible Deuteronomy will give you a better understanding of loveoutame and smartoutame,

These books talk about the issues surrounding the controversy of politics. But the books I am talking about have answers of how to stop the country from the kind of rituals they have been performing since their was a government.

It is time for us to stop being obsessed by the trump deranged sin-drome that the media has made so much out of.

To be downright truthful about the nastiness that has been portrayed by the new nominee if he becomes the new nominee, the fear and anger and madness that he shares that the kind like him feed off of has been such an obscene distraction it has presented itself whereas the devil has looked up out of hell to make sure that the others like him follow suit or else they may receive some kind of retribution of whatever nature or course they find themselves on as bodies of demonic obsessive towerists that has an evil statute in it. It is so unfortunate to witness this as someone who tries to help deliver people from this kind of ungodly negativity.

The only thing I have left to say about this information is God has anointed people in certain levels of life where their families will be blessed by the fruit and God has allowed curses on certain people and their families because of them choosing to follow Satan. What side do we all need to be on because you can get away with all kinds of hell. But in the presence of the Lord some day you will pay tremendously. Your family may wind up paying even more than you. It is the truth so let it be written and let it be told.

To come to a conclusion to a new beginning we have discovered many things about our issues in our society especially in America. The PTSD that service men and women have over the years that has caused them problems with suicide, etc. I have written a book to address this issue *The Unwounding of the U.S. Service Men and Women*. Now that the veil is off and we have opened up pathways of understanding what the problems are in our society and the overview of the governments PTSD that affects society as a whole we can now start to rejuvenate and cure these issues. One of the major aspects of helping this will be the next book, *The Comeback of America/2020*. We have more than enough to look forward to and be thankful for because we have now identified with these issues.

To add to it all to have some blessed kind of therapy and therapy comes from the truth we accept about our shortcomings as a nation of people and as a body of Christ and as humans. That is what is even more importance as we join together we do not separate we understand how to build and keep building while preparing to become a heavenly body on earth.

This is truly a part of the presence of being in the eye of a pleasant storm. That is where we are going in this country at this time due to all of the openness of the loveoutame process that is developing out of one thing, the God in me and out of you and out of everyone who is in the process of retooling the spiritual guidance and presence with these new kinds of skills.

The greatest thing to take away from this may be knowing that no one is 100% wrong in life. If you were the Lord would not let you be here. Some of us got a part of the one the Lord died to save us from and it is up to us to know the difference of what level we may need to untrap ourselves from, no matter how painful it may look like. It isn't that bad as it could become if you don't face it now the Lord answers parties of those that need answers to even if they didn't know they had a problem in the first place.

Proverbs 28:2, 6

If I am my brother's keeper then I should not let him hand himself down where he has his neck in a noose and give the end of the rope to Satan and he is slowly pulling him down into hell so he can drown in hellfire.

The bigger problem he has in the past for human Dem. or Rep. was them putting a noose around men's neck and openly hanging them and to a degree that is what he is still doing but he is causing others to do it to themselves in ways that are less obvious. It may sound ironic but some of the people went to their reward early thanks to them but their reward was do different.

Towerist

Therefore, do we stand up to the home grown terrorists we cheated in ourselves in our land. Now who will meet in the center to resolve the issue with themselves so it will not create one for someone else.

Does this process of thinking make sense if a towerist knows that it could be true they have a monkey or noose around their neck. Do they try to pave their way with others to go before them to hell by doing wicked things in darkness? Do they think subconsciously that Satan will give them preferential treatment? If so, I know the truth of denial may be there because of a spiritual sickness is there in them. If some don't know people need to check themselves before they wreck themselves. That is why this has been written to help stop the blindness of this kind of hellish people that the Lord's love because he is not a respecter of persons. He will treat us equal if we treat each other that way.

Therefore, is this someone working in darkness and know it is not known of themselves? If so, again if we can cut the noose to free them do we stop the people at the bottom who are less fortunate and at the same time the well off in the towers. I say yes again because the Lord isn't a respecter of persons.

73

The towerist has both traits: cynical and synical the second one has a new meaning. It is a person who may be afraid of telling the truth.

The placement of your heart in the truth of the wisdom you are not just learning but living on taking you to the sinoutame or crapoutame state of deliverance to help you get free of sin. It may not put you on the level of perfection but God knows you will be a better person.

God's therapy way

The process of what I am showing you is a spiritual lobotomy that detects the mental disorder along with some spiritual disorders. Can we think of someone after the fact has been lobotomized with the spiritual wisdom of the Lord. That repaired a backward way they may have been going that could have leads them to hell. I think so how about you?

Isn't it time you take a tripoutame to see the way to a better truth? You can see a better you with just saying I am seeing more of the Lord in me as I have learned to take a tripoutame to understand my personal sinectomy process and let it happen. Do this to eliminate the sin in me.

To understand this kind of dilemma bring new meaning to life with a new way to escape that they let all know the cost of the wages of sin has been paid up to date and it becomes more available to think along that line of reality in order to step more in line and less not being out of bound as Satan would like. Does this new way make sense to you to add it in your life. I hope so because it keeps making mine better and that is a fact.

The best is yet to come and it is based on one thing. That is right one thing and that is if we go forward by ourselves to get a personal relationship with the Lord this has to be and there is no other way.

The nuts that lead to the votes are out of control in ways that can't be seen. Not all people are nuts. The way I don't see is why I can't say what I feel. I feel that the people who want to think they are in control of others who are, for the most part, towerists.

The government has gotten lost in the way of every last president we have had, had a direct defect because of the way this country was started. It gives a development of the power to kill anyone who tries to stop the advancement of its agenda.

What do you think the effect on people is, if any? Well, it is a join to kill if you get in our way or we feel threatened by you.

Now can we look at the principles that curse the country it brought about the Civil War that took place on our homeland. What is the point? The effects of it does have a fallout. It is the GTPSD that blindly recruits the ungodly presence of death in the recruiting of what could be called the misguided people who are fed up with the government's illnesses. The demons of darkness places a sentence on them to join into Satan's dieconomie. There is an unknown truth that has to be known to help stop it.

How much of this is clear? I don't know but we will take whatever we get from it to save more lives.

Can it be a beginning to the steps to come down out of the tower by no. 45? I say this because in one of the books I authored, _Fixing What is Broken in America by Stopping Towerism_ I talk about the osmosis of Rapunzel with a man trapped in a tower wanted a fairy tale presence of Rapunzel to let down her hair so he can come down the golden stairs. Well enough about that but I look at no. 45's wife who went to the motherland and it gives me a sign of is she subconsciously let down the golden stairway in a Godly way to help lead her husband down out of the tower. Is this philosophy or idealism or pure spirituality speaking?

The better half has a better change to help someone then they may be able to help themselves due to a spiritual quest in a loveoutame for them process of growth.

Do we see that the towers that are still stuck together as shown in the Supreme Court nomination process that let someone who has the towerism in them up in the highest court in our land, it is wrong.

We already have a black sheep in there. Do we need another no matter what color they are? If we get another do we deserve it? I think not but what else have we got as Americans that we didn't deserve and if this is the straw that leads us to the needle that was found in the haystack. Let's use it to tie up some loose ends and put this country back together. The bottom line is we need to start wearing our top hat as voters.

We can get by the trump derangement sin-drome? To take the new ways of good that he has helped put in place for the country but it is not much more that we need to trust him with any longer as it is said he has hit it and let's help him quit it.

S-N

Don't be afraid of the harvest that is in the garden.

Now I think the no. 45 would be helped greatly with the book The power of knowing no also. It may give him a way out of wanting to build a wall that is only a kind of moral symbol that he feels or feeds on deep down inside of himself that he believes will protect the tower that he is in.

What can be some of the best ways to help people break the fears of coming down out of the towers? The books I wrote about the government can help. Always remember the Lord wants to keep us all safe in his bosom.

This is a type of protection through spiritual skills

The new book by Hillary Roden Clinton may help you gain additional insight about the political arena.

Taking it from the top

When you add up all the unnecessary death in the world it amounts to one thing. It is taken away from one of the thing the Lord told us to do be fruitful and multiply the earth. This was told to us because it is his way to multiply the heaven and no thanks to Satan's dieconomie. The process has been disrupted and that is why we need to put the newly sent word and it means the loveoutame process of a holistic healing way of a kind of breakthrough to a pathway on earth to a personal state of holiness. Any and all can enter. Amen and hallelujah!

The righteousness of being silver

It is time to cut the bull in half with the blue and red state and we look at things as a silver state plan to get the right thing done. I mean it would be nice to have a change made to whatever state there is that is willing to own up to their allegiance to the country to at least make the change of color to the state who has the right kind of silver lining in it for the people of the country and not just to stay with a political side because it remains loyal to the right or wrong it does.

So we bring forth the silver belt level of prosperity for the people even if it is only temporarily put in place to help show we can be lovers to the people in the country and not like those who spread propaganda.

There are a few paragraphs that are similar in three books to help broaden their understanding.

The better part is the ending of two kinds of spiritual warfare in the country that separates us. One the

people against each other and the politicians at war.
The killing and suicide, the abuse, the drug use, and
the list goes on. So to not bore you I have said
enough the ball is in your court shoot it or give it back.
Thank you, Bro. Bush in Christ that hopes we all see
that the ram is out of the bush and is not lost and
about Father God's business.

The 45th president has not yet brought forth the worse
level of GPTSD since the Vietnam War. He has put it
on the map again and we see what it did to people
before and that is what we are not willing to be a part
of ever again. Thank you Lord for watching over us.

  Let's get all we can get out of this part of a new start

Now we all have exactly what the doctor ordered.
What are we going to do with it?

Do you become cynical about this not thing you will
find wisdom or truth?

The loveoutame can bring the Shekinah glory out of
me and you also.

Philippians 1:27

Let's put ourselves in a thought process of Abraham
Lincoln and Franklin Roosevelt when they said we
can join together in our differences and so we can
make a meaningful end without destroying more of
the process of the American way than is needed or
than should be.

There is another degree of someone becoming a Galayif. They find themselves being bullied by a giant and a Goliath and they become a person of a mammoth's attitude and it projects fear in the party they are in such as what has taken place with the Republicans fearing that this man would be an enemy to them if they didn't bow down to him to present him as a justice if he got in not one wanted to share in with his anger that he used to bully and I believe he is guilty and is another black sheep in the courts of Supreme Justices.

If you find your life seems to be moving in a circle and you keep going around the same old thing and you keep going around the same old thing without making any progress in a spiritual way, you may want to look into reading the book of Judges to find the answers you need to start making progress to get straight up out of the same old scenario that brings no spiritual growth.

You can consider this healthy homework.

It is time for the politicians to stop acting like Pharisees, Sadducees and Scribes and understand what their responsibility and obligation was in the body of Christ and keep themselves in line with politicians and not try to be someone that is of a higher justice than they could ever become no matter how high they could be. This means nothing to the Lord because he is not a respecter of persons.

Here is the real deal. We are brothers' keepers. We teach them how to cut the rope or take the noose off their neck that Satan uses to pull them down into hell because being a tower they are pulling back and raising hell with in their towers where people are being affected all around them, no matter where they are in government or business, etc. if they are a towerist.

Little towerists have a noose around their necks also. We are teaching them how to not raise this hell that way less people are affected and they can become free from the bondage. What kind of paycheck do you get at the end of your life. Do you get a paycheck for being a hell raiser or do you go to hell or heaven or getting yourself a nice room in the mansion. That is the bottom line for you in this scenario dealing with the inner towerists.

This is a brief analogy of it all

When I first started writing this I don't think that I could take it because it took so long to make it and I will never this recipe again but all prays go to the lord for it completion.

I had to catch it when it came along because if I hadn't it may have been lost forever. It may have taken almost 100 lifetimes to get it done by someone in the first place so enjoy this privilege that the Lord has presented to us. I hope I can get as much out of it as you do.

Can this wisdom give a feel for the Proverbs in a way that reflects the meaning of an exegesis – explain or interpreting explanations of Scripture as being a cleric/cynicism. So can we not take it as a bad thing to get the trumpoutofme/towerismoutofme also. This book has been produced with a part of the loveoutame that was given to me by the Lord's loveinme.

Last comes first

Can this be some kind of safety measure that the Lord wants us to put in place to doge or get around and be forward about the invisible bullet or weapon the government is unwittingly using on its own people that has some people under friendly fire called GPTSD. It has been declassified and is no longer a covert operation that can harm anyone as is the non-towerist as a threat any longer.

Now can the no. 45 be the person to bring attention to the matter of stopping the GPTSD so that the Lord can bless the multitude out of bondage on many levels? Now can the wisdom you already have see the blessing in here for you!

Acts 20:24 – But none of these things move me; nor do I count my life dear to myself, so that I may finish my race with joy, and the ministry which I received from the Lord Jesus, to testify to the gospel of the grace of God.

Philippians 4:17 – Not that I seek the gift, but I seek the fruit that abounds to your account.